More Praise for Heart*Ignite*

"Debra Valentina is a woman who ... dous courage and passion. Her jourı ...pı∽ oı now we can transform ordinary adversity into a ...y∽ı ıor deepening our relationship with self and the world at large."
Debbie Pallett, MSEd, MS-PA-C
Physician's assistant and visualization coach

"Recounting years of life lessons and accumulated wisdom, Debra Valentina beautifully covers many of the foundational spiritual truths. This book is thorough, open, and intimate."
Kathyrn Russell, MA
Artist, writer, and therapist

"Reading this book was so nurturing for me. After reading it, I am dedicated to living an authentic life."
Pamela Wagher Donovan
Office and theatre administrator

"Debra Valentina brilliantly leads us step-by-step to examine our own beliefs that have shaped our lives. Through her own life example, we can courageously join her in choosing thoughts and beliefs that create a joy-filled life we all desire."
June Laraway, RScP
Chaplain

"Debra Valentina intimately knows what exquisite self-care feels, looks, and tastes like, and through this book she guides others to experience it in their own lives."
Devin Grace
Counselor and author of *Silence Whispers*

"Debra Valentina brings together a tool kit for living well and understanding our potential to determine the flow and heart of our lives. She communicates how our intention can be a source to identify and develop what we want and clearly deciphers the traps that keep us from full expression."
Cyd West
Vice President of Economic Development
Metro Phoenix Partnership for a Creative Community

"As you eagerly turn each page on your quest for abundant choices and miracle manifestations, Debra Valentina delivers a journey that you will embrace. Get ready to ignite your heart with the eternal flame of full expression!"
Dr. Pat Baccili
The Dr. Pat Show, #1 Show on VoiceAmerica.com

Heart*Ignited*

Living a Fully Expressed Life

Rebecca ~
May you always
live a fully expressed
life !
Debra

Debra Valentina

BOOK PUBLISHERS NETWORK

Book Publishers Network
P.O. Box 2256
Bothell • WA • 98041
Ph • 425-483-3040
www.bookpublishersnetwork.com

10 9 8 7 6 5 4 3 2 1

Printed in the United States of America

LCCN 2009921954
ISBN10 1-935359-09-6
ISBN13 978-1-935359-09-8

Heartignited® and Essence Statement® are registered trademarks of Heartignited LLC. Avatar® and Star's Edge International® are registered trademarks of Star's Edge, Inc.

Editors: Devin Grace and Julie Scandora
Cover Design: Effusion Creative Solutions
Typographer: Stephanie Martindale

I dedicate this book to my beloved Guardian Angels who have guided me with clarity and grace along my journey.

CONTENTS

Acknowledgements

I have been blessed to have so many human angels surround me throughout my life. I wish to name a special few who have assisted me in seeing some of the insights I share with you, the reader, in this book.

To my coaching clients, I deeply admire your courage and have learned more from you than I can possibly express.

Dr. G., I thank you for re-opening the doors to my feelings and to trust, once I thought I had nailed them shut.

Rita, I thank you for all of our profound "time line therapy" sessions in which I was able to create new outcomes to some old stories.

Sunil, I am grateful to you for leading the way to exploring different spiritual disciplines in order for me to find and walk my own path.

Kathy, I thank you for being such a perfect mirror so that I am able to see my reflection with more grace and ease.

Lisa, you are not only a dear friend from whom I always learn, you are a model of the divine and powerful feminine.

Devin, as friend, coach, editor, and angel, I am grateful for all of our playful learning together.

How to Use This Book

Perhaps like me you are fortunate and grateful to be a healthy, happy, and peaceful person who feels free and able (at least most of the time) to express yourself. Or perhaps that is your goal. The ability to self-express and the subsequent feeling of deep satisfaction does not happen magically. Some of you have spent many years or lifetimes on the quest to feel whole—I know I have. At this juncture of my own journey, I can honestly say I now understand that there is no need to get anywhere or do anything. Each one of us is already whole and complete. We always were.

We just have to *remember* that we know this. That is the purpose of this book—to spark that remembering until you no longer need reminders because you have absorbed it into your waking consciousness. With this *knowing* comes the freedom to experience, to experiment, and to contribute. When you do not have to prove yourself to anyone, including yourself, you can choose to experience whatever you want. What a feeling of freedom and joy this knowledge brings! It is like unlocking a magic door and feeling a cleansing, refreshing breeze sweep over you.

This book is designed as a workbook, and there are questions to answer and practices for you to "try on." It is written so that you may approach it at your own pace. You may choose to read it from start to finish and then go back to answer the questions and implement the practices. Or you may choose to take one chapter at a time and do the work within. For those of you who like to go right to the heart of the matter, there is a table of contents. You can choose a subject that resonates with you and begin there.

Each of the thirteen chapters encompasses "wisdom gained" gathered throughout my journey and illustrations of how I applied that wisdom to live a more fully expressed life. I am continually amazed at how the essence of these stories is so universal—I could tell dozens of similar stories from the lives of courageous clients.

The chapters all have a similar format. At the beginning are beliefs; an old belief I held that became no longer useful and the new beliefs I consciously adopted and put in its place because they were much more empowering. The essence of the chapter is then illustrated with examples from my life that may spark recognition of something similar from yours. Woven throughout are questions to prompt your thinking and feelings about the impact of these issues on you.

At the end are contemplation questions and practices offered to assist you in fully absorbing the chapter's message. You may want to choose a special journal for these practices or you may want to use the journal pages found at the end of this workbook.

My deepest intention is that you are served by this book. With that desire in mind I have changed some of the names of those I wrote about. However, all of the events occurred, and with the retelling of these stories, I am voicing them from my perspective.

Writing this book has served as a priceless part of my healing journey. If you are drawn to read it, I believe you will find gems in here that were meant just for you. May you be inspired to live a life of joy and full expression!

With love and blessings to each of you,

Debra Valentina
Spring 2009

Chapter One

My Beliefs about Beliefs

My Beliefs about Beliefs

Beliefs

Old Belief

- I know what *my* beliefs are and they are *the* truth.

New Beliefs

- My beliefs attract my experience.

- My beliefs are *my* truth and I can change them as I desire.

- It is easy for me to change my beliefs since it is I who created them in the first place.

Wisdom Gained

From a very early age, I have been a questioner. I was a questioning girl, and now I am a questioning woman. I was always questioning what was being told to me as *the* truth. While I was sitting in church at the age of five, our Presbyterian minister was talking about how we are all sinners, and I remember thinking, when have I had time to be a sinner at this young age? How would I know how to be one? What had I done?

At age twelve, after having gone through the required classes about how life is according to the Presbyterians, it came time to join that same church. I didn't want to, but not joining would have been unacceptable, particularly to my father, since he was an elder in the church and believed in its teachings so strongly.

So, being a dutiful daughter, I joined with all of the other coming-of-age girls and boys. I still remember my stomach being in turmoil for days during that time. To this day, my stomach is a good indicator of my state of Being and a real reflection of my

Knowingness knowing better. *Whenever my heart, mind, and spirit are not aligned, my stomach seems to be the first to know.*

- **When has your heart, mind, and spirit not been aligned? Where do you feel it in your body? Place your hand there for a moment and thank it for communicating with you.**

I have always been curious about other religions and beliefs. As a child, in addition to my Protestant friends, I had both Catholic and Jewish friends. I went to Communion service with my Catholic friends and often went to Saturday synagogue with one of my best friends, Judy. Judy was on the more orthodox side of Judaism, and so I would eat kosher with her.

I remember one particular holy weekend I slept at Judy's house, and the next day while making scrambled eggs, I automatically added milk to make them fluffier as my mother had done. After Judy got over the shock of my doing this, she explained to me that in her kosher world, eggs and milk were not to be mixed or cooked together.

Although I did not believe in her kosher ideology, I found it fascinating that her family's beliefs were so different from my own. I can see now that I was exploring what people believed and thus exploring what I wanted to believe and what made sense to me.

- **What are some beliefs that you grew up with that you questioned and still do? What are some of your beliefs from childhood that you now hold that you consciously chose to keep?**

When I left home for college, I began more actively to be a "seeker." I did not actually know what I was seeking, but I sure wanted to explore what was beyond *the* truth that was being espoused by my family, friends, and teachers. And in my late teens, my journey began in earnest.

As a college student I was fascinated with Maslow's "hierarchy of needs" and the studying of what needs have to be met in order to realize self-actualization. While many of my classmates were out drinking and experimenting with drugs, I took yoga classes, explored meditation techniques, and read Kahlil Gibran (a Lebanese writer who wrote inspirational poems and the book *The Prophet*).

At the time, it often felt lonely to be choosing to do what most others were not choosing. Yet I was compelled to explore spiritual concepts and that which is invisible yet knowable.

- *When have you chosen to go a different path from the majority? Did it result in what you wanted?*

As a management major in my undergraduate senior year, I went to New York City to shadow the chief operating officer of the mental health unit at a large urban hospital. During this administrative residency, I lived with about a dozen other students in a brownstone house in Brooklyn Heights.

I was the only student being mentored in hospital administration. Most of the others were in the arts (ballet dancers and artists), and my roommate was studying advanced sign language. Living with this group of young people with such diverse interests and worldviews served me in examining my own viewpoints and beliefs.

- *When have you surrounded yourself with others who had different viewpoints from your own? Did it affect your beliefs? If so, in what ways?*

A few years later, as a graduate student in healthcare administration, I went to the School of Public Health at the University of California Berkeley. I was able to learn about leading healthcare organizations in the broad context of public health. Even then, my *Knowingness* was interested in a wide perspective.

My classes were very eclectic and included such disciplines as public health, business, and law. I was particularly enamored with systems theory because it espouses the integration of many belief systems simultaneously.

In addition to my academic subjects, I also read books that expanded my spiritual awareness, and I had many opportunities to explore the mystical and unknown through some very aware professors. In addition to opening my mind to new ideas, I also opened myself to new experiences.

One of these experiences was presented by a professor who seemed often to test my beliefs about reality. One day he invited all of his students who were interested in experiencing massage to a private home.

Many students from our co-ed class showed up. When I arrived, to my shock and bemusement, everyone was naked. This "still naïve in a lot of ways" New England bred gal just stood in the entryway. After a few minutes, I knew I had to make a decision: leave quickly, or *just notice my belief that this was "bad and wrong" and take my clothes off!* I decided on the latter.

Although nervous, even though the massage was non-sexual in nature, I allowed myself to be introduced to the wonderful world of massage that afternoon. Some thirty years later, my body is still enjoying the relaxing and healing effects of massage.

- *What formal or informal education or training have you engaged in that has broadened your worldview?*

Shortly after I graduated from Berkeley, a girlfriend introduced me to the *est* training (now transformed into the *Forum* led by Landmark Education trainers). I was intrigued, felt urgency to participate, and took the training in 1980. For the next ten years I participated in the programs of Landmark Education which included becoming an "Introduction to the Forum" leader.

During this time, many of the indoctrinated beliefs from my childhood about how life worked were challenged. What I welcomed from my participation was the opportunity to create new beliefs and *to have my reality be shaped by what I said/ believed, not what I adopted from someone else.*

- *Who or what has helped you create your own beliefs for your life?*

In 1995, I took the Avatar Course, a nine-day self-exploration course created by an unassuming and brilliant man named Harry Palmer. I have been profoundly influenced by the Avatar Course and delivered it for a brief time in the late 1990s. One of the many things I have integrated from my participation in Star's Edge International (Harry's organization that created the Avatar course and other transformational courses) is the knowledge *that my beliefs really do attract what I experience* and that I am the one who has adopted or actively created my beliefs, and thus I am the one that can change them whenever I choose to do so!

You may be thinking "Oh, Debra makes this sound *so* simple," and I am here to tell you that it is this simple, as long as we are aware of what beliefs are operating. It is the beliefs that we are not aware we have that are the ones that trip us up. Often I find new beliefs that I did not know I had. The beliefs that attract what I want I keep and the ones that attract what I *don't* want I replace with beliefs that align with who I am now.

- *What philosophies have most profoundly affected your current beliefs?*

I believe that my thoughts and beliefs are extremely powerful in manifesting what I want and what I don't want. I believe it is essential for my evolvement to practice mastery over my thoughts and beliefs.

Contemplation Questions and Practice

If you wish, choose a quiet place to contemplate and journal the answers to the following questions:

- What is currently happening in your life that you don't like or don't prefer? What are the possible beliefs that are at work in attracting these unwanted situations?

- What new beliefs might you replace these outdated beliefs with in order to attract what you do want?

Then:

- "Try on" these new beliefs that you just created, as if you are trying on a new pair of shoes, and observe what comes up for you.

Chapter Two

Being Is Enough

Being Is Enough

Beliefs

Old Belief
- I am not nearly enough, and I need to do BIG things to prove I am enough.

New Beliefs
- My *Being* is enough.

- Who I *am* contributes to others.

- My outer world reflects the *knowing* from my inner world that "I am enough."

Wisdom Gained

I believe that *knowing* that I am enough has been one of the fundamental challenges for me in this lifetime. In the past I often found myself automatically asking: *"Am I doing enough? What else can I do to prove that I am good enough?"*

I grew up in a family of six. My parents had four daughters, all vying for attention of both mother and father, and particularly father who was not home much.

My father often forgot our names and referred to us as daughter number one, two, three, and four. Although he made a joke out of this, I know as daughter "number three" that it did not feel good to be referred to in such a generic way. I wanted to be acknowledged as a special Being, as I believe that is what we all are.

11

My father always wanted to have at least one boy and a successful boy at that, and I was happy to be that successful "boy" for him. I worked very hard to get stellar grades and then worked even harder to succeed in the "boy's club" of Healthcare Administration.

Despite my outward successes academically and professionally, I spent all of my childhood and way too much of my adulthood believing I was not enough. In fact, I spent over half a century trying to gather evidence that I was enough. I had always had a deep yearning to be "more" and was not sure what that "more" looked like, which led to my taking the *est* training, along with a very long list of other courses and workshops. From my experience as a life coach, I have seen that many women and men have their own version of the "not enough" story.

- *What does your inner dialogue say about your being enough, or not enough?*

Part of my evidence-gathering of "I am enough" included my academic training and leadership development classes. In my early thirties, I really wanted to be selected to attend the executive business program at Stanford University, a five-week program extending over a year. In 1984, I was thrilled when I was chosen from our health maintenance organization's (HMO) Northeast region to attend this prestigious program. I loved every moment of it and was in my glory being back in an academic setting, doing homework and participating in group discussions.

Even though I loved this experience, it still didn't fill me with the *sustained* feeling that "I am enough." That "I am enough" feeling only lasted a short time. I felt only momentarily satisfied and accomplished because it was an external indicator rather than an internal *knowing*.

- *When have you tried to prove that you are enough to yourself and others? What did that look and feel like?*

My ex-husband Gary would often say to me, "I feel as if I will never be enough for you or be able to do enough for you." I now realize that his feeling was a direct reflection of my feeling that I was not enough. I feel as if this is critical for me to remember and acknowledge, as I see this learning as an important part of my evolution and one that will not have to play out in my next long-term relationship.

In the last several years, I have created a new belief that "my *Being* is enough." What I mean by this is that just the fact that I am present on this planet is enough. I do not have to do anything, accomplish anything, or prove anything. For the majority of the time, I am able to live inside this new belief, and yet sometimes, I still slip back into the "not enough" story.

When I do slip back and then notice it, I do not beat myself up but rather gently coax myself back into my created belief that I am enough. Having this new belief creates an incredible amount of freedom for me to do, have, say, and *be* whatever I desire in any given moment. And I find that my "enoughness" helps me contribute more to those I come in contact with, whether that contact is for a few moments or on a daily basis.

- *Sit quietly for a moment and feel what it would feel like in your body to be enough.*

I believe that my belief "I am enough" is the most powerful belief I hold and that it is the foundation for my feeling satisfaction and joy in my life.

Contemplation Questions and Practice

You may want to set aside a few minutes to explore the following:

- Pretend that you must make a case to a group of your peers that you are "enough." What would you say and what examples would you use to make your "case"?

Then:

- Envision yourself peacefully sitting in front of that same group, not saying a word.

- Gently ask yourself: *Is it possible for me just to know that I am enough?*

Chapter Three

Authentic Success

Authentic Success

Beliefs

Old Belief
- Being successful means performing very well academically and professionally.

New Beliefs
- I know myself well and know what makes me feel successful.

- I know what I desire and what makes me happy.

- I am responsible for creating my own authentically successful life.

Wisdom Gained

When I reached my career goals in my early thirties, as an executive team member in a large HMO, to my severe disappointment and dismay, I did not feel satisfied or successful. I felt very angry.

- *Has there ever been a time in your life that your reality did not fit the pictures you created of your success story?*

I found myself lashing out at folks that did not deserve it. I remember the turning point when I knew that I needed professional assistance. One day when ordering art prints over the phone, I went ballistic on the salesperson when something went awry with the order. I felt completely out of control with my anger. Once I regained my composure and apologized, I went in confidence to Mary, the mental health manager at the HMO I worked for, and told her what had happened.

Mary immediately said that she would contact the chief psychiatrist at the Hartford Institute. It all happened very quickly, and for the next year, I was under the superb care of Dr. G., a traditional psychotherapist, which is what I believe I needed at the time, to start my more in-depth self-exploration.

What I began to realize was that my feeling of self-worth was totally connected to how I was performing at work. I so identified with being a healthcare administrator that if things were going well at work, then I felt okay, and if things were not going well, I did not feel good about myself.

During this time, things had begun to turn negative at work. My boss, the regional CEO, was at a six-month executive training, and she had brought in a temporary replacement. There were some very difficult issues at the health centers that I had never encountered before and that I was ill-equipped to handle.

Mr. Replacement CEO was not the mentoring type, and things did not go well. I needed a lot of assistance from Dr. G. to be able to make the distinction between myself as a human being and my identity as a healthcare administrator. Once I could make this distinction, it was life-altering.

After many talk-therapy sessions and lots of commitment and tenacity, I began to *feel* the difference between me as a sacred human being and me in my role as a healthcare administrator performing a very difficult job. I started to be able to distinguish myself (now I would say my *authentic* self) from my many roles and identities: professional administrator, volunteer, friend, spiritual seeker, etc.

- *What are the different roles that you take on in your life? Can you feel that these roles are distinct from you as a sacred human being?*

This "therapy thing" was a very vulnerable road to go down, oftentimes excruciatingly lonely and scary. My shining light at the time was my very fun and loving boyfriend Jean. I met Jean at the local Chamber of Commerce where he served as president of the board and I served as a board member. I remember having lots of fun and laughing with him more often than I had ever done previously in my life.

One of the beautiful things about being with Jean was that he was so complimentary about who I was as a human being. He made me feel valuable despite my being challenged in my professional responsibilities. Jean reinforced all I was discovering for myself in my sessions with Dr. G.

- *Who in your life mirrors the "true" you?*

At that time, I really needed Jean telling me how great he thought I was to in order to feel successful. Now I realize a feeling of *authentic* success only comes from within. However, having mirrors of that success from other people can be a true gift, especially when experiencing the roller coaster of life's challenges.

- *Do your feelings of success come from inside or outside of yourself?*

Meanwhile, I was gaining much more self-confidence from my work with Dr. G., and this was very timely due to my professional challenges. Upon my boss's return from her training, I negotiated an exit strategy for myself that included staying for several months while I found my next position.

Shortly after taking a position as CEO of a Pittsburgh-based health plan, I learned that the company that hired me had been bought out by a much larger insurance company. At this point, I already had some awareness that I was really an entrepreneur at heart and that this corporate world was not my cup of tea. I began, once again, planning my exit—this time to start my own business. So in the spring of 1987, my healthcare manage-ment consulting practice was born.

- *Have you ever had surprises or disappointments in your professional life? What did you learn that brought you closer to feeling authentically successful?*

Starting a company, with my own successes and failures, was the beginning of my living a more authentically successful life. And now I am in my current career of choice as a life coach, writer, and speaker, and living in my place of choice (the Califor-nia Coast) with a broad circle of friends of my choice.

My definition of *authentic* success is different from what I imag-ined it to be as a young adult. What now provides me with a sense of satisfaction and success is living by my own beliefs and values and contributing to others. I am grateful I stopped to *examine* what I really *wanted* to be doing.

I believe authentic success means living by my own beliefs and values that I have created or adopted by choice.

Contemplation Questions and Practice

You may want to find a comfortable place to examine these questions:

- *What is your definition of authentic success?* Take some time to contemplate your own definition and write it down.

- Create a vivid story about your authentically successful life. *What exactly does it look like? Who shares this life with you? What are you doing professionally? What activities are you engaged in? Who and what are you contributing to? What is the overall feel of your life?*

Then, if you desire:

- Make a "dream board" that represents your unique story.

  o Supplies needed: large white poster board, variety of old magazines, glue stick.

  o Flip through the old magazines and see what images resonate with you and cut them out as you recognize them.

  o After you have accumulated all the images that you desire, arrange them on the white poster board the way that feels good to you.

  o When you are done arranging, paste all the images down.

  o You may want to put this "dream board" in a place that you can see often as a reminder of what you are creating as *your* authentic success story.

Chapter Four

Head or Heart?

Head or Heart?

Beliefs

Old Belief
- My mind is more valuable than my heart.

New Beliefs
- My mind is a mighty and useful tool.

- When my heart is open, all is well.

- My head and heart make powerful partners.

Wisdom Gained

For most of my life, I have lived "in my head." It felt safer than living from my heart, and as a result, I believe I have had too much reliance on my mind. I still find that my "monkey mind" is omnipresent, an often loud and vivid commentator on what and how I *ought* to do things and, actually, how *all* things *ought* to be.

As a result of spending so much time utilizing my mind, I have a really good handle on logic and reason. However, for the majority of my life, I protected my heart. Now with daily practice, my heart is coming out to feel and express itself!

- *How much do you rely on your mind? How often are you living from your heart?*

In 1991, at age thirty-seven, after five years as a consultant, I decided to try the corporate world again. To start and maintain my business, I had borrowed more money from the bank than I was comfortable with. I felt that I could repay it more quickly by having a job with a consistent paycheck. I also thought that if I found a position that allowed for an independent role, I could be happy in this environment.

I accepted a position based in Chicago for a large preferred provider organization (PPO). Management hired me to negotiate contracts with physicians in order to develop a national physician network. For most of my tenure, I really loved the job, as I was in charge of my own mini-division within the company.

Within two years, I had hired thirty-three staff, and together we had negotiated more than twenty-eight thousand physician contracts. This accomplishment was not without its toll on me. At times, I was in three different cities in a week, and my body was weary from all the travel.

I had a lot of success at this company and was in line to get a significant promotion. However, as in my previous corporate jobs, there were policies and politics that were difficult for my entrepreneurial spirit to deal with. Because of this misalignment with my nature and my fatigue, I chose to leave.

It was not an easy decision to make because my head said that it was a good and well-paying job and to stick with it even if I was miserable doing it. My heart was saying I was going to get sick if I kept doing what I did not want to be doing and at the pace I was doing it. I am very grateful that I chose to listen to my heart.

- *When have you chosen to listen to your heart? Are you happy you did?*

One of the things that I used to do often was worry. I would find a reason to worry and then wait for "the other shoe to drop." A while back I figured out that worry did absolutely nothing to assist any situation, but nevertheless, my mind was on automatic pilot with the worry thing.

Recently I made a very useful distinction: worry comes from my head, not from my heart. So, if I am listening to my heart, I am not worried. This distinction has freed up my attention and energy for more creative and joy-filled experiences. *When I listen to my heart, I am in a "worry-free" zone.*

- *What is your relationship with being worried? Where do you find your "worry-free" zone?*

Another recent discovery I have made is that when I am in my head, I tend to be more serious and even stern, and when I am coming from my heart, I am much more playful, which I know is expressing more of my true essence. My practice now is to tap into the passion, creativity, and playfulness of my heart, rather than solely relying on my mind.

I believe listening to my head and heart is a potent combination. My mind and heart create balanced and grounded decisions.

Contemplation Questions and Practice

You may want to sit in a peaceful place for this practice:

- Identify a major decision that you currently want or need to make.

- Ask your mind to talk to you about the pros and cons of your options. Next, *feel* into your heart and see what it has to say. Are your head and heart in agreement? If not, which option feels more fulfilling to you?

- Is there a *new creative choice* that satisfies both your head *and* your heart?

Chapter Five

Health through Healthy Boundaries

Health through Healthy Boundaries

Beliefs

Old Belief

- I do not want to have clear boundaries because they inter-fere with my getting close to people.

New Beliefs

- I define and create my own healthy boundaries.

- I create my boundaries to be as strong or as flexible as I want and need them to be.

- My healthy boundaries assist me in creating intimate rela-tionships with others.

Wisdom Gained

Establishing healthy boundaries has been another challenge for me. This stems, in part, from my strong identity that I am a "nice person" and I want to be close to people. In the past when it came down to being a nice person versus holding a strong boundary, "nice person" almost always won out.

- *In what areas or with whom do you feel you have main-tained healthy boundaries? In what areas or with whom do you feel you still have some unhealthy boundaries?*

When I became the leader of a Pittsburgh HMO, the move hap-pened very quickly. Several days after the move, I was lonely and wondering, "*What have I done? I do not know one soul here!*" It was a reality that hit me hard.

Within the first week after my arrival in Pittsburgh, being determined to find connection with human beings, I phoned the local Landmark Education office to inquire about what evening seminars (Landmark offers graduate seminars in most major U.S. cities and around the world) were being held in the area. As it turned out, that evening the *Excellence* seminar was being offered just a few blocks away from the hotel that was my temporary home. I did go to the seminar, and it was an evening that altered the course of my life, as Sunil, my second husband, was at the seminar.

In Landmark seminars, there is always plenty of time to share, and share I did that night. When I was called upon, I was handed a microphone. I took it and explained that I had just arrived and that I did not know anyone in Pittsburgh. At this point, I began to cry, and it seemed as if I was crying *really loudly* into that microphone. I was mortified that I was emoting in front of all of these strangers. What I see now is that what I really wanted was for people to know and like me so that the intense feeling of loneliness would subside.

Meanwhile, in the back of the room, Sunil listened to my story and saw me in a very vulnerable state. I was planning to make a quick exit at the end of the evening, but I never did. At the end of the seminar, I looked up and saw that a line of people had formed to introduce themselves and to offer to be my friend, including Jane, who introduced me to Sunil. In this instance, not really knowing where my healthy boundary lay, what to share or not to share, worked to my benefit.

- *Where have you taken a risk and gone beyond your comfort level with your boundaries? How did it turn out?*

Sunil and I started out as friends, became more than friends, and married three years later. Our marriage started out pretty balanced contribution-wise and morphed into a lopsided arrangement. By the end of our fourteen-year marriage, I was earning the lion's share of the household income, handling the majority of the house matters, and was the instigator and planner of our social life.

It was not until I was completely exhausted from all of this and chose to leave the marriage that I finally realized how lopsided it had become. I remember my coach asking me, *"What will you do with all of your free time now that you are not doing everything in your marriage?"* It was one of those questions that riveted me and certainly made me stop and look at the reality that I did have *a lot* more time and energy. In hindsight, towards the end of this marriage, I had almost no boundaries: healthy, strong, or otherwise.

My definition of a healthy boundary is knowing what *feels okay* and what *does not feel okay* and knowing when that "not okay" line is crossed. I was not really *feeling* very much at all towards the end of our marriage, just *doing*.

- *Where in your life do you have lopsided arrangements with others?*

We are all different, and as a result where the boundaries lie is different for each of us. I believe boundaries can be flexible and move as we grow and evolve. What was once not okay may become okay; and what was once okay, may not now be okay. That was certainly true for me in my second marriage. What was once acceptable and even joyful for me, such as planning all our social events, had become unacceptable.

I know I can create my boundaries to be as strong or as flexible as I want and need them to be.

Contemplation Questions and Practice

You may want to sit in your favorite quiet place and then:

- Feel into your heart to identify an area in your life where you have a history of weak boundaries where you desire stronger ones; or identify a person with whom you have weak boundaries with whom you desire stronger ones.

- Experiment with holding a strong boundary in this area or with this person for at least a week. Notice when you hold firm to your boundary or when you allow it to be penetrated.

- When you feel ready, journal the answer to these questions: *What am I learning from observing myself in this practice? How may I want to change my behavior?*

Chapter Six

Core Essence Clarity

Core Essence Clarity

Beliefs

Old Belief

- My core essence needs to be expressed in a particular way.

New Beliefs

- I continue to awaken to the many aspects of my core essence.

- I decide how I express my core essence at any given time.

- My core essence will always involve serving others.

Wisdom Gained

I believe that we all have a unique core essence that wants to express itself in the world. I also believe that there are many different potential expressions to our individual core essence and that, as we mature, we may become aware of those multiple aspects, like facets of a unique gemstone.

To define and gain clarity regarding our core essence, we can start by asking: *what are we deeply passionate about and what are we really, really good at?* Where the answers to these questions intersect will point us in the direction of our core essence (an analogous idea for companies called "The Hedgehog Concept" is described in the book *Good to Great* by Jim Collins). Currently, one facet of my core essence expressing itself in the world is as *a coach committed to empowering women to fully express themselves.*

I spent over thirty years of my professional life expressing another aspect of my core essence: contributing to the U.S. medical care delivery system by being a healthcare executive and owner of three healthcare-related companies. At the age of three, I had made a decision that affected this career choice.

While I was in the hospital for an infection when I was three, I was placed in a baby's crib. I said to myself, "How dare they put me in this when I am way past the crib stage!" I distinctly remember feeling outraged at my treatment, and what followed was my forming a strong opinion that "these hospital people have got to do better than this," and then I envisioned myself running hospitals. I later proceeded on that path.

- *What opinions/beliefs do you hold that have affected the expression of your core essence?*

In the second year of my Berkeley masters program, we had a requirement to work as an administrative resident. To my complete delight, I was chosen as a six-month financial resident at a California-based HMO. Within a year after my residency, I was offered a position as assistant administrator for a hospital in that system. I loved my job and was thrilled to be able to provide vital medical care services for the community. At that time, my core essence was expressing itself in the way I had envisioned as a young girl.

- *Where have you felt your core essence shine?*

My own experience, as well as my experience as a life coach, tells me that people's expression of their core essence may be connected to an issue they feel is unjust, unfair, or "not right," or it may be something that has brought them joy for as long as they can remember.

A situation that I wanted to "correct" came at age three when I was in the hospital and thought to myself "I can do better than this"; and *voila*, I aspired to and became a healthcare leader for thirty years. Something that has always brought me joy is being of service to others, like my coaching practice does now.

- *What has inspired the expression of your core essence? Where have you felt your core essence change expression?*

I believe that my core essence integrates what I am deeply passionate about and what I am really, really good at. I also believe that I have many aspects to my unique core essence.

Contemplation Questions and Practice

If you wish to get clearer about your unique core essence, you may want to journal the answers to the questions below with your non-dominant hand. If you are right-handed, write with your left and vice versa. Writing with your non-dominant hand allows you to access your feelings and creativity more easily.

- What am I deeply passionate about?

- What am I really, really good at?

- Keeping the answers to the above two questions in your heart, create a short phrase that captures the aspect of your *core essence* that you are experiencing now. For example, the aspect of my core essence that I am experiencing now is: *I am a coach committed to empowering women to fully express themselves.*

Chapter Seven

Keeping Attention on Intentions

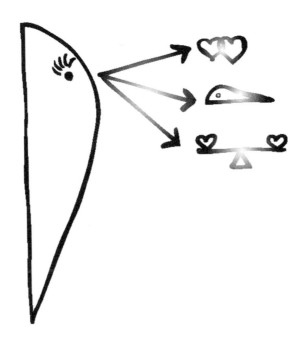

Keeping Attention on Intentions

Beliefs

Old Belief

- I have an unlimited amount of attention and energy to do all the things I want to do.

New Beliefs

- I have access to a specific amount of attention and energy at any given time.

- I am clear about my intentions in order to align my attention, energy, and actions behind them.

- What I focus my attention on is what I will create.

Wisdom Gained

I have always had lots of interests I wanted to explore and, gratefully, had the ability to focus for long periods of time on ones that especially captivated me. While growing up, those things included homework, art projects, and practicing my flute.

As a child and teenager, I was stimulated by and got deeply involved with academic homework in my room. My attic bedroom was my sanctuary, my safe haven to dive into my interests without interruption. It was where I could put all my attention on whatever project I chose.

In addition to studying, I loved just about anything that had to do with art. In grade school, I was into designing clothes for my Barbie doll. At one point in grade school, we had an art teacher in addition to our regular classroom teacher, and I cherished that art time.

- *As a child and young adult, what did you put your attention on?*

After a long period of not painting, I am once again focusing some of my attention on art by experimenting with watercolor and pastels. It works like a charm to put me on the creative side of my brain, which is in alignment with my intention to express creativity in many areas of my life.

As an adult, what I believe is that I have a certain amount of attention in any given day, week, month, or year. What is very powerful is to be clear about what I intend to create and then to align all of my attention behind it. Currently my intentions lie in the areas of serving my clients, living in a healthy way, having fun, traveling, and writing and speaking about full expression.

- *What are your current intentions? How much of your attention is devoted to these intentions?*

For the past thirteen years, I have been actively paying attention to where my attention is going. This discipline has eliminated some habits that I once spent time on. For example, I no longer watch or listen to news that upsets me, I no longer spend time with acquaintances that drain my energy, and I hire out for those activities that I am not good at.

Early on in my consulting career, I had little awareness of where my attention was going, and as a result, I wasted my attention on endeavors, such as researching potential diversification areas that I really had no intention of pursuing and spending time with potential clients that I knew intuitively would not turn into business.

For me, freed up attention translates into energy that I can use to create more of what I want and to contribute more to others. *Keeping attention on my intentions is one of the most fundamental and powerful tools I have to create the life I desire.*

- *Where in your life do you feel you may be squandering your attention?*

One way I have created more attention is by getting rid of all the "shoulds" in my life. It still amazes me to find so many "shoulds" lurking around despite declaring a "should-free zone" several years ago. As soon as I notice a "should," I question whether or not I truly want or need to do it.

- *How many "shoulds" do you still have in your life?*

My belief is that what I focus my attention on is what will manifest. The first step to creating the life I desire is to become clear about what I want. For whether I am doing it deliberately or not, I create my reality, and I want to create that reality with clarity!

Contemplation Questions and Practice

Here are some practices you may want to experiment with:

- Declare a "should-free zone" for yourself for a week. Every time you think or say, "I 'should' do x or y," question if you really *want* to do x or y, and then deliberately choose to do it or not based on your wants.

- If you wish, the following week, ponder what your top three priorities are for the next six months. Create clear intentions for each priority. For example, a *priority* might be "to create a healthier body" and an *intention* might be "to eat only when my body is hungry."

- Ask yourself if you are committed to having your attention on these priorities until you create them. If you decide you are committed, start focusing your full attention on them and watch them manifest!

Chapter Eight

Abundant Choices

Abundant Choices

Beliefs

Old Belief

- There is only one "right" choice for me and I need to discover what it is.

New Beliefs

- I always have an abundant number of choices that are "right" for me.

- I decide what choice will work for me.

- All my choices lead to my highest and best good.

Wisdom Gained

Throughout my life I have made choices that would not have been expected given my family history. I became a healthcare executive, entrepreneur, and coach instead of becoming a teacher. I live in the West, California now, Arizona and Washington before that, rather than in the East where I was born. I was the first one in my family to get a divorce, and then another divorce!

- ***Where have you made unexpected choices given your background?***

In any given situation, I used to think that there was only *one* right choice. I remember agonizing over the "big" choices such as which graduate program to participate in, whether or not to get married to my first husband, whether or not to stay in the corporate world, etc.

I had several choices of where to go for my healthcare administration degree. I narrowed my final two choices to the University of Michigan and University of California, Berkeley. One evening during my deliberation, I received a call from Peter, the Berkeley healthcare administration head at that time. He told me that the Berkeley administrators thought their program would be a good fit for me, and in addition, the school was offering me a public health scholarship. I happily accepted the offer, and it was the beginning of my belief in serendipity!

At the same time, I struggled over whether or not to get married to Gary. I met Gary on a blind date in my junior year in high school, and we dated for seven years before making a decision to get married. We argued often. However, I did love him, so I made the decision to marry him a year after I completed my undergraduate degree.

In my early twenties, I had little self-confidence, especially regarding relationships with men. I thought that it was the right choice to marry Gary because I thought it was the *only* chance I would have to get married. Of course, in retrospect, I ask myself, "*What was I thinking?*" Now my viewpoint is very different. *I believe we all have abundant choices and that every choice will lead us to our highest and best good.*

- *Where have you thought that you only had one choice?*

Gary and I loved one another, though, as I said, we disagreed frequently. In retrospect, I was looking to Gary to make me feel whole and complete. I now realize that it was not his responsibility and that only I can do that for myself. We decided to divorce five years after we married. One aspect of our parting that I am most proud of is how we *chose* to divorce. The divorce was not without pain. However, it could have been more difficult, as many divorces seem to be.

I remember going to a friend, a corporate attorney, and she advised me to get a divorce attorney right away. Gary got the same advice from those closest to him. Both of us consulted one another and decided we would stick to our original plan to make it as simple as possible, to file ourselves, and to split the cost. That is what we did and it cost each of us $37.50 to get our divorce in California in 1983.

We divorced with dignity and grace, despite all the voices around us giving their viewpoints which I believe would have resulted in just the opposite. I feel the commitment to do it peacefully was an outward manifestation of our love for one another and is still a *choice* I am proud of today.

- *When have you been proud of a choice you made that may have been counter to what others were advising you?*

In 2005, out of my belief that I always have choices, when I felt complete with my thirty-year healthcare career, I was able to transition easily to coaching and writing. Also in 2005, when Sunil and I divorced, we chose to do it with respect for each other, and to this day we remain supportive of each other even though our marriage is dissolved.

Believing in abundant choices allows me to see multiple options in each situation, and this belief opens up the gateway to my creativity and gives me a sense of boundless freedom.

Contemplation Questions and Practice

You may want to curl up in that cozy spot of yours and contemplate the following:

- Where in your life do you believe you have limited choices or no choice? Then ask yourself if you are willing to "try on" this belief: *I always have choices.*

- While you are trying on "I always have choices," journal about your options regarding the issue you have identified. Be open to surprise regarding the multiple scenarios that may appear!

- Then when you are inspired to do so, choose one option that surfaced while journaling and act on it. Observe what happens from your action(s).

Chapter Nine

Exquisite Self-nurturing

Exquisite Self-nurturing

Beliefs

Old Belief

- Only when my needs get loud enough should I take care of them.

New Beliefs

- Listening to my needs is essential for my well-being.

- Taking exquisite care of myself feeds my body, mind, heart, and spirit.

- Taking exquisite care of myself provides me with the energy to serve others.

Wisdom Gained

As early as age five, I began working hard in school and at home. I can remember vacuuming the house furiously to make the carpets and floors clean. We lived in a very modest duplex house in western Massachusetts. My father had started out working in a paper mill and later became a graphic arts union president, and my mother worked as a sales clerk in a retail department store.

One belief that was very ingrained in our family was that "you work hard to get anything in life." It was part of the Protestant ethic that had been passed on for generations. My paternal grandfather was a self-trained engineer and was an evening shift boiler watchman in a factory. He was also a self-taught watch repairman and fixed watches on the side. My paternal grandmother worked on an assembly line on the evening shift.

On my mother's side, my grandfather worked in a Pennsylvania steel mill most of his life, and when he "retired" he did a variety of odd jobs, including cleaning a movie theatre well into his seventies. As you can see, I come from a long line of hard workers, for which I am grateful. However, there was not much attention, if any, placed on self-nurturing, never mind *exquisite* self-nurturing.

My maternal grandmother, Gramsy, worked in a variety of blue-collar jobs. The ones that I remember were picking rhubarb at a very early age and later on in life being the cook at Horse Happy Farm, a vacation retreat for equestrian young adults.

Gramsy's last job as a school cafeteria worker was with a specific objective in her mind, a trip to Hawaii. She attained that goal and took her daughter and two youngest grandchildren, my younger sister and me, to visit four of the Hawaiian Islands. It felt like an exotic trip as a teenager and out of the ordinary for our hard-working family tradition.

- *What beliefs did you grow up with regarding nurturing yourself?*

For many reasons, I looked up to my maternal grandmother, and one of them was that she loved to laugh! Her laughter was very contagious, and I laughed a lot with her. I found back then and to this day that laughter is an elixir for my soul and definitely self-nurturing. Most often I can find humor in whatever is going on, no matter how challenging. As I get more and more in touch with my playfulness, I find myself laughing out loud, even when I am by myself.

- *What makes you laugh? Does laughter nurture your soul?*

When I was young, my mother, three sisters, and I spent two weeks each summer in Myerstown, a small eastern Pennsylvania town where my maternal grandparents lived. I still remember it as the happiest and most freeing two weeks each year. It was the one time that I recall letting myself relax and not work so hard.

As an adult, two weeks of vacation a year is not nearly enough to sustain my body, mind, heart, and spirit. Some time ago I consciously decided that self-care and nurturing are critical. Self-care now includes dancing solo to my favorite music, massages, hot bubble baths, pedicures, painting, reading a good book, long chats with my friends, eating well, taking my vitamins, exercising regularly, getting enough sleep, and treats such as lattes and chocolate. Exquisite self-care also includes a respite from my mind with a minimum of twenty to thirty minutes of quiet time or meditation each day.

- *How do you nurture yourself or allow yourself to be nurtured?*

For most of my life it never occurred to me that non-physical activities such as positive self-talk, versus negative self-talk (thoughts about not being enough), are just as important, if not more so, than a massage. Also, second-guessing myself had, until recently, become a very bad habit.

This second-guessing myself is the *opposite* of self-nurturing. For the most part, I have overcome this, and it is mainly due to my coaches who told me pointblank to "stop it!" And just recently, after getting *really* sick and tired of doing it, I am finally getting the message.

Now I find it amazing to observe my mind on automatic pilot, chattering away on some program of self-flagellation. I call this my "monkey mind," and when I want to quiet it gently, I visualize feeding it a banana. *I have learned that the more I resist the chatter, the louder it gets,* so feeding it a banana occupies it and switches its attention from me to the banana!

- *How often do you second-guess yourself? How often do you hear your "monkey mind" on automatic pilot?*

I believe I am like many women in that I have a strong tendency to take care of others, and often forget to take care of myself. I will say, however, I am getting pretty good at self-care these days. I have found that in order to have enough energy to enjoy life and to serve others the way I desire, my own tank must be filled up.

I believe that exquisite self-care is essential for my well-being and know it feeds my body, mind, heart, and spirit. Taking exquisite care of myself provides me with the energy I need to serve others.

Contemplation Questions and Practice

To further your ability to nourish yourself, you may want to engage in the following:

- For a full week, envision something different to do each day to take exquisite care of yourself and practice nurturing yourself in those ways.

- On the seventh day, for the entire day, ask yourself, "*What do I want to do?*" and then do that. When that is done, ask yourself, "*What do I want to do now?*" and then do that! Notice how you feel throughout the day. You may want to journal about how you felt yourself shifting during this pampering week.

- As a celebration of your shifts, dance to one of your favorite pieces of music. *Feel* the music and *flow* with it.

Chapter Ten

Dancing with the Feminine and Masculine

Dancing with the Feminine and Masculine

Beliefs

Old Belief

- I get more rewards for expressing my masculine energy than for expressing my feminine energy.

New Beliefs

- My feminine and masculine energies dance in harmony with one another.

- Expressing the full range of my feminine and masculine energies is what I truly desire.

- My contribution to others comes from full expression of both energies.

Wisdom Gained

I have spent much of my life expressing my masculine energy: driven, directive, results-oriented, competitive, and structured. As I spent much of my time in my masculine energy, I realize now that I was suppressing my feminine energy.

These days I love when I allow myself to be in my feminine energy: flowing, fluid, flexible, creative, and spontaneous; and even to experiment with my feminine flirty side now that I am single again. While growing up, being in my softer feminine energy was most noticeable to me when I was in my art moments: drawing, painting, and designing clothes.

I believe that we human beings, both females and males, have a wide range of feminine and masculine energy that we can choose to express at any given time.

I believe the height of my expressing my masculine energy came while I was an HMO administrator in Connecticut from 1983 through 1986. Looking back at it now, I was expressing way more masculine energy than feminine energy.

I was responsible for turning around one nearly failed health clinic, opening up another one, as well as making plans to expand the health plan into New York and Massachusetts. The amount of driven and focused energy those duties took was enormous, and I became totally exhausted. My feminine side did not feel nourished by the intensity of that focus and drive.

- *When have you spent concentrated time in your masculine energy? What project(s) were you engaged in?*

Kauai, Hawaii, is known for its feminine energy, and the island feels soothing to me in every way, from the soft breezes that blow to the gentleness of the Islanders' voices. It felt very easy for me to write there when that feminine creative energy was surrounding me.

As I am recently awakening to a fuller expression of my feminine side, I am enjoying it tremendously. I moved to the Pacific Northwest for a couple of years beginning in the fall of 2006. My friend Kathy introduced me to a body of work called "WarriorSage," self-evolvement work developed by an inspiring man named Satyen Raja. As I view it, his work is about experiencing the full range of masculine and feminine energy.

While I was living in Pittsburgh, I spent much time with my dear friend Mary. To me, she was a role model for expressing feminine sensuality and sexuality. Mary owned a women's clothing store with gorgeous fashions, and I trusted her to pick out flattering clothes for me. I remember one particular outfit: a pink silk flowing skirt with a blouse to match that I loved and wore often. I now believe the reason I loved it so much was that it expressed my repressed feminine side.

- *How much time do you spend in your feminine energy? What does it look and feel like when you are in your feminine energy?*

In 1985, while living in Connecticut, I decided to reconnect with my old boss and mentor from the University Health Center. Michael was brilliant at what he did, and I felt very attracted to him. So in one of my rare "feeling feminine" spontaneous moments, I called Michael up and told him I was coming to Chicago. He invited me to stay at his apartment downtown. I accepted and off I went. I spent about a week, and everything about that trip fulfilled my fantasy of how it would be with him.

We saw each other a few other glorious times. I did not seem to have any trouble expressing my feminine energy when I was with him. I believe that while Michael solidly held the place of the masculine, I felt safe in expressing my feminine more fully.

- *Who or what brings out the feminine energy in you? Who or what brings out the masculine energy in you?*

We all have ample opportunities to practice expressing a full range of masculine and feminine energy. Sometimes a situation calls for me to be in my masculine energy, as when negotiating the purchase of a new car or focusing on a project; and sometimes it is fun to express my feminine side, as when dancing my heart away or changing my mind over and over again!

I love the flow between feminine and masculine energies. My intention is to dance in harmony with both my feminine and masculine energies.

Contemplation Questions and Practice

You may want to call upon your creative self and journal the answers to these questions:

- How broad is my range of feminine and masculine energy?

- How do I express both? Is there balance or imbalance between the two energies?

- If there is an imbalance, how can I begin to create more balance between these two distinct energies?

Chapter Eleven

Work and Play Harmony

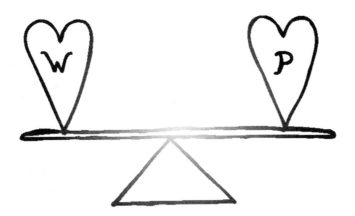

Work and Play Harmony

Beliefs

Old Belief
- How hard I work proves how worthy I am.

New Beliefs
- I am worthy.
- A balance of work and play is healthy.
- I am a playful woman.

Wisdom Gained

For the majority of my life, I have been mostly about work. Now I find that I create a lot of play. In fact, I experience life as full of play; even my work feels like play. My experience with my coaching clients is that many women are about working hard and keeping multiple balls in the air, making little time for play.

- *How much play do you allow yourself? Do you desire more play?*

How did I go from mostly work to lots of play? I believe I learned this lesson by experiencing periods of nearly total burnout.

In 1995, Sunil and I moved to the Southwest. We had honeymooned in Scottsdale and Sedona and had always dreamed about leaving the cold of Pittsburgh for a warmer climate. Sunil found a job at a start-up software company based in Scottsdale. Soon after, I met Steven, my future business partner. Steven was a creative guy who had developed a holistic mental health program that worked with people who went to the doctor often yet did not seem to be getting any better with the frequent visits.

Steven and I began working together at first long distance and then in Scottsdale when we moved. The tricky thing was that there was only enough money being generated to pay Steven and his research assistant. I worked nearly full-time at our start-up company for sweat equity, so I decided to earn money on the side by re-starting my management consulting practice.

While marketing my consulting services, I met Martha, a woman who had started a networking group for professional women in healthcare. Shortly after, Martha asked me if I would assist her with organizing the meetings, and I said yes; and soon after that, I became president of the organization for seven years. Thus, in 1996, I was juggling three major career pursuits: an entrepreneurial business, a consulting practice, and leading a professional organization. There was no work-play balance in this arrangement.

- *When have you found yourself out of work-play balance?*

Fast forward to 2004, nearly ten years after we had arrived in the Southwest, I was consulting full-time and was now the major breadwinner since Sunil had been laid off his technology job. Bottom line, I was on the fast track to *really* burning out.

I am a real "doer" and believe that I will choose to remain as such, given all the things I want to contribute in this lifetime. But there is such a thing as *way* out of balance, and I was on that trajectory. One day while speaking to my coach, I decided I had had enough and that I needed just to *stop* and re-evaluate the "doingness" of my life.

Now in 2009, I am happy to share that, much of the time, I experience work-play harmony in my life. I love coaching, writing, and speaking, and I make lots of time for play.

- *How often do you experience work-play harmony?*

The harmony between work and play means what *feels* healthy. Since I did not experience much play in my childhood, I am committed to having more of it now in my middle years and beyond.

We may not always experience harmony on a daily basis; instead, we may create it over a period of time. I still go through periods of intense work like writing this book, and intense play such as taking a sabbatical between my management consulting practice and coaching career.

Creating work-play balance is an ongoing practice. I listen to my mind, heart, body, and spirit and know that they will always tell me when harmony is missing.

Contemplation Questions and Practice

If you wish and when you feel ready:

- In a gentle tone, ask yourself: *How shall I begin to incorporate more work-play harmony in my life?* Jot down your ideas in your journal.

And then:

- Ask yourself, *What is the very next baby step to begin creating the harmony I desire?*

- Take that one small step in the next week to create more harmony for yourself.

Chapter Twelve

Simplifying Life

Simplifying Life

Beliefs

Old Belief

- The more complex I make life and then manage it, the more I prove I am intelligent.

New Beliefs

- I am intelligent.

- Clarity provides simplicity.

- The simpler I create my life to be, the more satisfied I am.

Wisdom Gained

I used to think being able to handle complexity in my life was a badge of honor and proof of how intelligent I was. Of course, since I did not believe that I was intelligent enough, I relished all the proof I could get. Thus I created complexity in my life and a great deal of it.

Until the last several years, I was handling multiple professional jobs at the same time. Even when I was focusing on my consulting practice, I was working on many projects simultaneously, and each one of them was something new. I prided myself on giving my clients tailored responses to their specific needs.

As a result, I was essentially re-inventing the wheel with each new healthcare client. While this stretched my brain tremendously, it also took a great deal of energy and created a lot of complexity. With each passing year, it seemed as if the ante was raised, and the projects got more and more complex.

After my Chicago PPO job, I took a much needed break for a couple of months and went to India with Sunil. He had been hired as a systems consultant for a South Indian steel plant in a place outside a city called Vishakhapatnam, or Vizag for short. It was quite the adventure. For about a month I traveled with Sunil's mom, sister, and nephew all across North India while Sunil worked in South India. For the last month, I stayed in a beautiful hotel in Vizag and lived like a queen.

There was a gorgeous pool at the hotel, and it was scrubbed each morning by a man with a little hand-held scrub brush. This man dove under the water as long as he could hold his breath, came up for air, and dove back down again. The pool was spotless. For me, this morning scrubbing ritual was a demonstration of simplicity. I also noticed the contrast that while this man scrubbed the pool, I sat in my lounge chair with my feet up, sipping my juice and coffee that had been served to me without my asking.

From my vantage point, India is a country of extraordinary simplicity and, at the same time, extraordinary complexity. The contrasts of simplicity and complexity I experienced in this country were fascinating to me. In 1993, while I was being served abundant and delicious meals by servants, three million adults and children lived on the streets of Calcutta—as many people as those who populate whole cities throughout the United States. You did not have to look very far to see people washing, nursing babies, cooking, playing, and just plain living on the street. I never heard the word "homeless" in India; it just seemed like a fact of life that there were millions of people without shelter.

- *Where have you witnessed simplicity in action? Where have you witnessed complexity in action?*

When I returned from India, I went back to consulting, and I still attracted complex projects. One of *the* most complex was as a subcontractor to a large mental health plan, which provided the care in multiple Arizona counties for those that could not afford it. I was first hired to oversee and "manage" the old vendor that had several months left on its contract.

When the mental health plan had an urgent need to sign contracts with providers and facilities, my client asked me to handle the negotiations within sixty days. Never backing away from a challenge, I said yes, and so, in addition to my management responsibilities, I proceeded to close the deals. I am not sure the situation could have gotten any more complex or stressful than this.

When my portion of the project was complete, I *finally* began to think about this complexity issue. *Why did I attract such complex and stressful projects? What was my ego getting out of this, and what rewards did I get from doing these crazy-making assignments?*

By inquiring, I began to see that my ego was very involved in my attracting these ever more complex situations. My ego got to prove that it was smart. This epiphany came in 1997, and I have spent the years since then unraveling my complex life and simplifying it. There was much to unravel.

- *What are you attracting into your life – complexity or simplicity?*

So I have unraveled much of the complexity in my professional and personal life. As much as possible, I impose a "should-free zone" in my life. This one intention adds hugely to making my life simpler. Instead of seeing how complex I can make life, I see how simple I can create it. The simpler I can make my life, out of the complex circumstances this modern world has to offer, the happier and more authentically successful I feel.

- *Which areas in your life would you like to simplify?*

I play a fun game with myself by frequently asking: *how can I make this challenge or project simpler? How can I do this with less effort?* Just asking these questions activates my creative juices, and I almost always come up with a more direct route to wherever I am trying to go. These questions train my mind to take the most direct and simplest route to the result I desire.

I believe that clarity gets to the heart of the matter and provides simplicity. I know that the simpler I create my life to be, the more satisfied I am.

Contemplation Questions and Practice

As soon as you start a new project or come across a challenge, you may want to ask yourself:

- How can I make this simpler? How can I do this with less effort?

Then:

- Make a choice to follow what your mind comes up with, as it will encourage and train your brain to follow a simple path with other challenges.

- As you practice the above, notice if there is a shift towards the direction of more ease and simplicity in your life.

Chapter Thirteen

Freedom in Self-expression

Freedom in Self-expression

Beliefs

Old Belief
- Fully expressing myself would be too much for myself and others to handle.

New Beliefs
- By being fully expressed, I have much to contribute to the world.

- I have an enormous capacity to express myself.

- Speaking and acting honestly is an expression of true freedom.

Wisdom Gained

I now experience my life as free on many levels. For me, some of the most important aspects of this freedom are my freedom to choose, freedom to love, freedom to *Be*, and freedom to be free.

A crucial part of my journey has been learning *to listen to my own Knowingness*, and the sense of freedom derived from listening to it is exhilarating. I believe my sense of freedom comes from being able to think my own thoughts, not just indoctrinated or reactive ones. It is not that I do not have reactive thoughts or indoctrinated beliefs; in fact, I experience them all the time. *The difference is that now I notice them and then I choose to do something, or not, about them.*

- *How often do you listen to your Knowingness?*

Speaking and acting honestly is a daily practice for me. It is so easy for my ego to run the show. I have become very vigilant about being cognizant of who is speaking to me – is it my ego or is it my *Knowingness?* Learning to tell the difference between the two is not always easy.

My ego is usually in a hurry, and it answers my inquiries in an urgent and sometimes frenetic manner – and this is not who I want to be listening to! My *Knowingness* has a quieter, more subtle, patient, and peaceful tone. That more peaceful voice is the one I want to listen to.

- *How does your Knowingness speak to you?*

I feel equipped, with all the practices and new beliefs described in this workbook to continue to explore a life of full expression as my journey continues. I now *know* I am whole and complete just as I am, and the practice for me now is the moment to moment remembering that I do know this!

Yes, there is more to learn, more to improve upon, yet there is nothing fundamentally *wrong* with me and everything fundamentally *right* with me. What this wholeness means for me is that I have a great deal to contribute to the world. There is much to be done.

While in Kauai, I spoke with a lovely family of four (mom and dad and two very articulate boys), and we began chitchatting about the state of the world. The mother remarked that there were so many issues in the world to fix. I responded, "How great! Now it is just a matter of choosing which one you want to contribute to and *go for it!*"

- *Where do you want to contribute in the world?*

In addition to my professional work, one of my favorite ways to contribute to the world is to volunteer as an activist and fundraiser for The Hunger Project. I have been actively involved with this amazing and highly effective organization for twenty-nine years. The Hunger Project is a strategic organization that partners with the chronically hungry people of the world in the areas where it persists the most: South Asia, Africa, and Latin America.

One of the many things that I love about this organization is that it knows that one of the key ingredients to ending hunger on our planet is to partner with women and men to end their own hunger and poverty. Partnering in this way makes me feel as if I am empowering myself and my fellow human beings, as well as fully expressing what I am desiring for myself and the world.

I believe knowing that I am whole gives me the freedom to turn my attention outward to assist in making this world a better place.

Contemplation Questions and Practice

You may want to take some time and savor answering these questions in your journal:

- What is my definition of freedom? Does it involve self-expression? What else does my definition entail?

- Am I experiencing the degree of freedom I desire? If not, what can I begin to believe or start to do now that will change that?

Then:

- Take one small step this week, and then every week, for the rest of your life, that will shift you in the direction of more personal freedom and your vision of full self-expression.

Notes

_____

_____

_____

_____

_____

_____

_____

_____

_____

_____

_____

_____

_____

_____

_____

_____

_____

_____

Heart*Ignited*

Notes

_____

_____

_____

_____

_____

_____

_____

_____

_____

_____

_____

_____

_____

_____

_____

_____

_____

_____

_____

Notes

_____

_____

_____

_____

_____

_____

_____

_____

_____

_____

_____

_____

_____

_____

_____

_____

_____

_____

_____

Heart*Ignited*

Notes

_____

_____

_____

_____

_____

_____

_____

_____

_____

_____

_____

_____

_____

_____

_____

_____

_____

Notes

Heart*Ignited*

Notes

_____

_____

_____

_____

_____

_____

_____

_____

_____

_____

_____

_____

_____

_____

_____

_____

_____

_____

_____

Notes

_____

_____

_____

_____

_____

_____

_____

_____

_____

_____

_____

_____

_____

_____

_____

_____

_____

_____

Heart*Ignited*

Notes

_____

_____

_____

_____

_____

_____

_____

_____

_____

_____

_____

_____

_____

_____

_____

_____

_____

_____

Notes

Heart*Ignited*

Notes

_____
_____
_____
_____
_____
_____
_____
_____
_____
_____
_____
_____
_____
_____
_____
_____
_____

Notes

Heart*Ignited*

Notes

_____

_____

_____

_____

_____

_____

_____

_____

_____

_____

_____

_____

_____

_____

_____

_____

_____

_____

Notes

_____

_____

_____

_____

_____

_____

_____

_____

_____

_____

_____

_____

_____

_____

_____

_____

_____

_____